HOW TO GET PAY FOR SOME OR ALL OF YOUR LONG-TERM CARE EXPENSES...

without having to wait 5 years.

without having to sell your house.

without having to go broke first.

(a Florida Medicaid Lawyer's Guide for Non-Lawyers)

6TH EDITION

Jason Neufeld, Esq.

www.ElderNeedsLaw.com

Central Scheduling (throughout Florida):
(786) 756-8169

More Free Educational Content can be found on our YouTube channel: https://www.youtube.com/@elderneedslaw; or on our website: https://www.elderneedslaw.com/blog

TABLE OF CONTENTS

INTRODUCTION

Much to the surprise and dismay of many, **Medicare** only covers short-term care and a maximum of 100 days in a rehab or skilled nursing facility. It can be quite a shock when clients' families realize that when Medicare stops paying, they will be faced with the prospect of exorbitant long-term care costs. Also, long-term care starts way before a nursing home is needed – usually in-home health care aides come first, then an assisted living facility may be needed. Finally, when 24/7 care is appropriate, you or your loved one may benefit from (or require) a skilled-nursing facility.

From hiring a home-health aide, to paying for assisted living facilities or skilled nursing home care, five years of long-term elder care can easily cost between $200,000 and $600,000. These costs threaten to completely decimate the life savings of many elder Floridians.

Most people don't realize that **Medicaid** can be made available to pay for long-term-care expenses. Many more are confused as to how to apply. Misinformation abounds about having to wait 5 years to apply, or whether Medicaid will go after their children's assets, or even having to sell their home.

Given the amount of misinformation being disseminated about Medicaid, and who can obtain its valuable long-term care benefits: this guide seeks to provide clear steps to enable you to better understand the resources available for you to better care for your elderly or disabled loved ones.

Gaining a more thorough grasp of how to navigate these support systems ultimately results in having additional resources to improve one's quality of life.

What is Medicaid Planning?

Medicaid planning is essentially the process of legally and ethically shifting assets from the status of "unprotected" or "countable" - to the status of "exempt" or "non-countable" - in order to qualify someone for Medicaid long-term-care benefits at home, in an ALF, or in a nursing home.

These benefits will greatly alleviate the immense costs of long-term care, thus preserving assets for the Medicaid recipient and the well spouse/community spouse – allowing both to have access to additional resources and have a higher quality of life.

Ultimately, Medicaid Planning makes it more likely that assets will remain to be passed onto heirs.

There is usually more than one way to make one Medicaid eligible. Your "Medicaid Planning Lawyer," "Medicaid Lawyer," "Elder Law Attorney," or "Elder Care Lawyer," (these are all slightly different ways of describing the same type of lawyer) will present you or your loved one with several options along with a pros and cons analysis of each.

Our clients are usually excited and relieved after we explain our Florida Medicaid-planning strategies.

Is Medicaid Planning Unethical or Somehow Cheating?

No. Medicaid planning, done properly, is all above-board, legal, and ethical.

Most people do not realize that Medicaid is not just for the poor or impoverished. Generally, my clients who need Medicaid planning are middle class folks who have savings. In fact, they have mostly saved their entire lives for retirement, only to be shocked and dismayed at the incredibly high cost of long-term care.

For those who worry about the ethical implications of Florida Medicaid Planning, I always ask: consider what you would do if you were ultra-wealthy?

It's no secret: the wealthy meet with tax attorneys and accountants to utilize EVERY LEGAL LOOPHOLE available to minimize what they must pay – to preserve as much of that wealth as possible.

This is what elder law attorneys do – except my colleagues and I are protecting the assets for people who don't have millions of dollars in the bank. Elder care lawyers who focus on Medicaid planning are simply taking existing state and federal laws and applying them to benefit their clients – to shelter assets legally and ethically in a way that makes them eligible to receive assistance from the government.

I am exceedingly proud of what Elder Law Attorneys can accomplish for our clients. I argue that when a multimillionaire saves a couple hundred thousand dollars by utilizing the tax code to their advantage, it typically results in a rather less-significant impact to the millionaire's life compared to when I can shelter a couple hundred thousand dollars for my elderly or special needs client – who only has that amount to live on!

Not only is Medicaid planning, when done right, completely ethical, and legal, rest assured that nothing is hidden from the government. In fact, Medicaid-planning lawyers tell Medicaid (or Department of Children and Families, which is the government agency that determines whether or not an applicant is eligible for Medicaid in Florida) exactly what it is that they are doing with the applicant's assets – and then explain how, under Federal and State law, our client still must be granted access to valuable long-term care and health insurance Medicaid benefits.

DISCLAIMER

This book is **not** designed to substitute for the advice of a Florida Elder law attorney who focuses on Medicaid Planning. Every case is unique and warrants a review by a qualified Medicaid lawyer. In fact, laws are always subject to change, and different community Medicaid offices may be stricter or more lenient with the level of scrutiny they will place on Medicaid-planning strategies. **You should never attempt any of the techniques described without the supervision of an experienced Medicaid lawyer.**

In addition, by design, I am trying to keep this book short. It is not a legal treatise or a detailed explanation of the law. Certain concepts are only touched upon (and the ones that I do address will have exceptions - and exceptions to those exceptions - not discussed here), and some are not addressed at all.

Instead, this Medicaid book should be used as an informational guide only for the layman. Essentially, it will allow you to educate yourself on common Medicaid concepts and allow you to ask more intelligent questions when you sit down with a Medicaid lawyer, who will then go over the entire Medicaid-planning process in much greater detail.

My real goal, by writing this book, is to help you become a better advocate for yourself or the person you are trying to help.

Finally, I am only licensed to practice law in Florida.

While Medicaid is a federal program, the individual states are provided discretion in how they apply eligibility standards. As an example, the "personal services contract" (discussed in Chapter 5) is a strategy that can be used in Florida – but not in many other states.

It is always important to consult with an elder law attorney in the state in which the eventual Medicaid applicant lives. If you, or your loved one resides in Florida (or are considering a move to Florida), we invite you to consult with our office.

**Central Scheduling (throughout Florida):
(786) 756-8169**

ADDITIONAL RESOURCES

I have created www.ElderNeedsLaw.com as a community resource. It is frequented by many visitors, including elder care, estate planning and probate lawyers, looking for clear explanations on these important topics.

We also offer FREE webinars on Florida Medicaid Planning and Estate Planning (available on the website: www.elderneedslaw.com/webinars)

I also address questions by video on our YouTube page:

www.youtube.com/@elderneedslaw (or just type in "elder needs law" in the YouTube search bar).

You'll find the video content immensely practical and educational (if you agree, please share, and subscribe to the channel).

New articles and videos are added frequently to the site on topics ranging from: Medicaid Planning, Estate Planning, Probate, Medicare Supplements, and Life Insurance.

I hope you enjoy this book and I wish you and your family good health and prosperity.

CHAPTER 1.

BASIC MEDICAID QUALIFICATION CRITERIA

FIRST - SOME IMPORTANT MEDICAID NUMBERS

I put these "important Medicaid numbers" at the top of Chapter 1, because, while they may not make much sense to you now, I will explain them later in this book. So, you can always refer back to the beginning of Chapter 1.

(as of January, 2024 | these numbers periodically change)

1. Income Cap: $2,829.00 (gross)

2. Asset Cap: $2,000.00 for an individual/$3,000.00 for a married couple.

3. Gift Penalty Divisor (average monthly cost for nursing home care in Florida): $10,438.00

4. Personal Needs Allowance: $160.00 per month

5. Community Spouse Resource Allowance (CSRA): $154,140.00

6. Minimum Monthly Maintenance Needs Allowance (MMMNA): $2,465.00

7. Maximum Monthly Maintenance Needs Allowance: $3,854.00

8. Home Equity Limit: $713,000.00

Medicaid applicants must meet certain criteria in order to be approved. The first set of standards requires the applicant to be a US citizen (or legal permanent resident for at least five years), and to be a resident of the state in which the Medicaid application is being submitted.

My practice is limited to Florida, so this book refers to Florida Medicaid qualification standards, only.

WHAT IS MEDICAID?

It is useful to understand that "Medicaid" is not just one program.

Medicaid is actually an umbrella term that refers to multiple programs. Most Medicaid programs are a Federal and State partnership, where the federal government sets standards and provides significant funding, while the state is given some latitude on eligibility standards and administers the programs.

This book is primarily focused on the Florida Institutional Care Program (ICP) and the Home and Community Based Services Program in Florida (sometimes referred to as the Florida Medicaid Waiver program, which has a waitlist).

There are other Florida Medicaid programs, such as MEDS-AD, Medically Needy, and Medicare Savings Programs (QMB, SLMB, and QI1), that have different income and asset requirements than the primary focus of this book. In Chapter 9, I will further describe some of these lesser-known Medicaid programs.

This book assumes that the applicant is already medically qualified (i.e. they currently need assistance with their activities of daily living).

To qualify for Medicaid's long-term care benefits (through its Institutional Care Program, or a Home and Community Based Services program), the applicant must meet both Medicaid's Income and Asset Tests.

MEDICAID INCOME TEST

As of the publication of this edition of the book (2024), each Medicaid applicant in Florida must gross less than $2,829.00 (this number changes every year) per month from all sources combined, in order to pass the Medicaid Income Test.

If the applicant's total gross income exceeds this "income cap" they are not Medicaid eligible, unless the excess income is transferred into a Qualified Income Trust (also sometimes referred to as a "QIT," a "Miller Trust," or a "d4B" Trust). Most elder law attorneys who handle Medicaid planning matters will be well familiar with drafting and establishing Qualified Income Trusts.

Qualified Income Trusts will be discussed in more detail in Chapter 2 of this book.

MEDICAID ASSET TEST

In addition to meeting income-test criteria, a single Medicaid applicant must also have no more than $2,000.00 in total countable assets. A married couple, if both want to qualify for Medicaid, can have no more than $3,000.00 combined.

What is, or is not, considered a "countable asset" will be discussed in more detail later in this book - as will strategies used to convert countable assets into non-countable or exempt assets.

Rest assured, most clients go to an elder law attorney with significantly more than $2,000.00 in assets, and we will present multiple ways to protect those assets and still get them qualified for Medicaid.

RULES TO PREVENT WELL-SPOUSE IMPOVERISHMENT

The government recognizes it has an interest in not forcing well-spouses (often referred to as the "community spouse," because it refers to the relatively healthy spouse who is able to live independently in the community; and not in need of assistance with their activities of daily living) into poverty so that their sick or disabled counterpart can receive government assistance.

Community Spouse Resource Allowance

If you refer to the Important Medicaid Numbers section at the beginning of the chapter, you'll see a reference to the Community Spouse Resource Allowance (CSRA).

The CSRA becomes important to satisfying the Medicaid Asset Test, if one spouse needs long-term care assistance while the other does not (so only one spouse would be applying for Medicaid).

In this situation, Medicaid allows the community spouse to keep up to the CSRA in countable assets in addition to the $2,000.00 asset test limit imposed on the Medicaid applicant.

As a simple example, as of January 2024, we know that the CSRA is $154,140.00. If the couple has, together, no more than $156,140.00, they would be able to satisfy the Medicaid Asset Test. Medicaid would disregard the CSRA as well as the Medicaid applicant's $2,000.00 asset cap limit.

Unfortunately, the CSRA does not apply to single/widowed Medicaid applicants, who remain limited to the $2,000.00 asset cap limit.

The CSRA also does not apply if BOTH spouses require Medicaid services (in which case, the spouses could have no more than $3,000.00, combined!)

Minimum Monthly Maintenance Needs Allowance

While the CSRA makes it easier for a married couple (with one spouse applying for Medicaid) to satisfy the Asset Test, similarly, the Minimum Monthly Maintenance Needs Allowance (MMMNA) can help that same couple satisfy the Medicaid Income Test. However, the MMMNA is a concept only utilized when the Medicaid applicant is looking for institutionalized/nursing home care.

The MMMNA (as of January 2024) is $2,465.00 per month.

The MMMNA rules allow the sick spouse, in a nursing home, to divert sufficient income so that the community spouse can keep his or her income and divert a portion (or all) of the Medicaid spouse's income in order to meet the MMMNA.

As a simple example, suppose the well spouse receives $1,000.00 from social security each month (with no other source of income) and the spouse applying for Medicaid receives $2,000.00 from social security each month. The well spouse would be able to keep 100% of their income and receive $1,465.00 of the Medicaid spouse's income so that the well spouse earns the MMMNA.

This means that the Medicaid spouse would only have to contribute $535.00 toward their nursing home "cost of care," and Medicaid would cover the rest ($2,000.00 - $1,465.00 = $535.00).

The Medicaid applicant would actually get to keep an additional $160.00 through their personal needs allowance (a subject we haven't covered yet, but I wanted to keep the example simple).

In addition, the community spouse would likely be able to keep an additional sum of the Medicaid spouse's income to cover certain shelter expenses.

As a reminder, the ICP program is what pays for skilled-nursing facility care.

If the Medicaid applicant were applying for help paying for home-health care or the cost of an Assisted Living Facility (ALF, which is different than a skilled-nursing facility), you or your loved one would NOT apply for ICP. Instead, you/they would apply for the Medicaid Waiver program – different rules apply.

For home or ALF assistance, your Medicaid lawyer would not go through the same minimum monthly maintenance needs analysis because the Medicaid recipient (if eligible) would keep all their income (whether or not some of it needed to filter through a Qualified Income Trust) and receive extra assistance from Medicaid.

This is an important distinction to reiterate and keep in mind: Only in a nursing home, rehab, or LTC facility setting does Medicaid require a substantial portion of one's income to go to the facility.

In an assisted living facility (ALF), independent living, or home care setting: the Medicaid recipient keeps and will continue to utilize 100% of their income for their care or other needs.

Again, remember, Medicaid is comprised of different programs: the two that pay for long-term care are Institutional Care

Program (ICP) or Medicaid Waiver (a/k/a "Home and Community Based Services" or HCBS Medicaid).

There are additional Medicaid programs that aid with non-long-term-care purposes, which are not the primary focus of this book.

<u>BIG TAKEAWAY</u>

Medicaid is really an umbrella term that refers to multiple different types of program.

The two that we will focus on mostly are:

1. Medicaid Waiver/HCBS (helps pay for home-health care and ALF care)

2. ICP (helps pay for rehabilitation, nursing home, skilled nursing care)

These long-term care Medicaid programs have a unique asset and income test (and strategies to assist those who are not initially financially eligible), which do not apply to other Medicaid programs.

CHAPTER 2.

MEDICAID INCOME TEST AND THE QUALIFIED INCOME TRUST

As briefly mentioned in Chapter 1, one does not qualify for Medicaid if they earn, from all sources combined, more than the income cap, which is tied to 300% of the SSI Federal Benefit Rate (or $2,829.00/month as of January 1, 2024).

As the federal benefit rate increases, so will the Medicaid Income Cap in Florida.

Please do not confuse IRS income rules with Medicaid income rules.

Medicaid income eligibility also has nothing to do with your expenses. In other words, being unable to save money due to important and valid living and/or medical expenses is, for Medicaid long-term care eligibility purposes, irrelevant.

In addition, items you are used to deducting from gross income must still be included for Medicaid Income Test calculation purposes.

For example, premiums for Medicare taken directly from Social Security, premiums for other health insurance policies, and premiums for life insurance policies are still included in Medicaid's gross income calculation (i.e. you must add those deductions back in).

For example, if you show me the Medicaid applicant's bank account statement that shows monthly social security deposits of $2,700.00 per month, $2,700.00 is NOT the number used when doing the income-test calculation -- because the dollar amount that hits your bank account does not include the Medicare Part B premiums that are automatically deducted from your Social Security check. In other words, the income that hits your bank account is "net" income and Florida Medicaid Long-Term Care Programs (i.e. ICP and Medicaid Waiver) are interested in "gross" income.

You are, in fact, obligated to add the Medicare Part B premium back when counting "gross" income.

Not only that, but Florida Medicaid also wants to see evidence, from all income sources, from the source itself.

Even if a Medicaid applicant's only source of income is Social Security, the applicant must produce their actual social security benefits verification letter (proof of income letter) from the Social Security Administration, which will show the gross income amount prior to any deductions.

In 2024, the typical Medicare Part B premium is: $174.70 (it is higher in some cases). So, in our above example, assuming no other sources of income, our hypothetical Medicaid applicant's gross income would actually be $2,874.70 (which slightly exceeds the income cap limit, thus requiring a Miller Trust).

Some sources of money are not counted as income for Medicaid purposes. Reverse mortgage payments and home equity loan payments are not counted as income, but if retained in the following month, will be deemed assets.

Similarly, if the Medicaid applicant borrows money on a valid loan, the proceeds are not income the month they are received but are considered an asset the month after.

However, most every other consistent influx of funds is counted as income for Medicaid eligibility purposes. All the Medicaid applicant's income sources will be added up to determine whether income exceeds the income cap limit.

For example:

Social Security Income (i.e. before Medicare Part B deductions come out)

+ Retirement account distributions (i.e. 401(k), IRA, etc.)
+ Pension payments
+ Other dividend and interest payments (unless de minimis)
+ Annuity payments
+ Investment Income (e.g. stock dividends)
+ Rental Property Income
+ Alimony received
+ Veteran's Pension payments (excluding amount for Aid and Attendance, Housebound Allowances, or unreimbursed medical expenses)
+ Workers' compensation payments
+ (most any other source of active or passive income)
= TOTAL GROSS INCOME

Typically, I don't see such a long list of income sources. It is more common for a potential client to come to an elder law attorney with social security income alone, or social security and one other source of income (usually coming from a retirement account such as an IRA paying out distributions or pension).

When total gross income, from all sources, exceeds the income cap limit, Federal law will only allow the Medicaid applicant to satisfy the income test by placing the excess income in a Qualified Income Trust each month the Medicaid recipient's income exceeds the income cap limit.

Let's discuss: what, exactly, is a Qualified Income Trust?

QUALIFIED INCOME TRUST (QIT) = MILLER TRUST = INCOME-ONLY TRUST

"Medicaid Income Trust," "Qualified Income Trust," "Miller Trust," "Income-Only Trust"... these are all terms that mean the exact same thing and can be used interchangeably.

Take a very typical example: Mr. Smith has $3,000 in gross monthly income, but his nursing home costs $11,000 per month!

His income exceeds the Medicaid income cap, so Mr. Smith is ineligible to apply for Medicaid ICP benefits. But, he also does not earn enough to pay the steep nursing home bill.

So, he needs a Miller Trust.

Here is how to determine how much money should go into the qualified income trust each month: By utilizing a QIT/Miller Trust, we can qualify Mr. Smith for Medicaid by placing slightly more than $171.00 per month ($3,000 - $2,829.00) into the Qualified Income Trust.

We advise slightly overfunding the QIT to provide a cushion for any deviations in income from month-to-month.

In fact, some people find it easiest to just regularly deposit all of their income into the Miller Trust – especially if they reside in a nursing home to avoid having to do math.

How to Open a Qualified Income Trust Account?

A qualified income trust (QIT) should be drafted by your Medicaid planning lawyer. Then the trustee brings the fully-executed document to a bank to open a qualified income trust bank account (literally, just an account in the name of the QIT).

The Medicaid applicant's existing checking account, which receives social security, pension, and any other income can usually be set up to automatically transfer excess income, as it is received, into the new Qualified Income Trust account.

From the QIT account, the trustee will write a check for the personal-needs allowance either to the Medicaid recipient's personal account (or to the nursing home where personal accounts are often opened for residents to use for things like haircuts and other niceties). The trustee can also write a check to the spouse if there is an income allowance per the MMMNA in a nursing home / skilled nursing facility setting.

The Miller Trust trustee will then disburse all remaining amounts toward specified health insurance costs, special medical services, and the remainder to the skilled nursing facility.

> As an aside, I recognize that setting up and managing a trust can be daunting. Make sure you lean on your elder law attorney to provide written and verbal instructions.
>
> Our office provides an easy step-by-step guide for administering QITs to our clients and remains available to answer all Miller-Trust related questions.

If the Medicaid recipient is living at home or at an ALF, they will keep their income.

If instead of residing in a skilled-nursing facility; you or your loved one is in an Assisted Living Facility or wanting to receive care at home, a Qualified Income Trust may still be necessary.

However, in an ALF or home setting, the Florida Medicaid recipient keeps their income. While a portion of income may be required to pass through a Miller Trust, money will go in and come right back out in the same calendar month.

QIT funds can pay the assisted living facility or be put towards health and other medical expenses while the Medicaid recipient is living at home (e.g. additional home care or therapies).

Very specific instructions on how this works will be provided by your Florida elder law attorney.

QIT/Miller Trust – General Limitations

1. The Medicaid applicant/beneficiary cannot also be the trustee. The QIT trustee(s) can be anyone (spouse, family member, trusted friend) except the Medicaid recipient.

   Professional trustees are also available at an additional cost.

2. QIT/Miller Trusts must be irrevocable.

3. QITs are only to be funded with the Medicaid applicant's income (no other assets).

4. The State of Florida/Agency for Health Care Administration, retains a lien on all Miller Trust funds that remain in the QIT Trust upon the death of the Medicaid recipient – up to the amount of funds Medicaid has paid for the Medicaid recipient's long term care. This is referred to as the Medicaid Pay Back or Medicaid Estate Recovery.

a) However, since the account should essentially "zero out" by the end of every month (money going into the QIT just comes right back out to either go to the nursing home or pay for the Medicaid recipient's other costs of living), this shouldn't be much of a concern.

ANOTHER IMPORTANT QUALIFIED INCOME TRUST LIMITATION

The primary drawback to the Qualified Income Trust is that the income placed into the QIT can only be spent on medical/health-related expenses. If the Medicaid applicant is in a skilled-nursing facility or an ALF, this is usually not an issue.

However, when my client is seeking help paying for care at home, depending on monthly income amount, it is possible that they will run out of health/medical-related expenses (especially if Medicaid is paying for the bulk of their home attendant care needs).

An alternative to the QIT is a Pooled Special Needs Trust (PSNT).

A PSNT can hold assets as well as income. Because a PSNT can receive income as well, it can serve the same purpose as a QIT.

For income purposes, the only benefit to a PSNT is that this device does not have the same spending restrictions as a QIT (e.g. a PSNT can pay a Medicaid-beneficiary's property taxes, utilities, internet, credit card bill, and many other non-healthcare related expenses in addition to being spent on medical or health related services).

However, the PSNT must be managed by a professional trustee (who charges a relatively small fee).

Utilizing a PSNT is also useful when a Medicaid Applicant does not have anyone that they "trust" to be the trustee of their QIT.

The pooled special needs trust is discussed further in Chapter 6.

Do I use the beneficiary's social security number, or do I need an EIN when opening an income trust account?

It is proper to establish the Miller Trust Account using the SSN of the beneficiary since the income is solely that of the beneficiary.

Some banks will require a new EIN for the QIT, even though IRS rules specify that this not necessary[1]. However, the issue is not worth arguing about, so if the bank requires an EIN, that is easy enough for your elder-law attorney or accountant to obtain rather quickly from the IRS (it literally takes five minutes on the IRS website).

Your Medicaid/Elder Care Attorney will have much more detailed instructions to properly establish and fund a qualified income trust.

Experienced elder care attorneys usually have relationships with local banks so you can open the QIT account with little delay.

MOST COMMON MILLER TRUST MISTAKES

There are some common mistakes and misconceptions I routinely encounter.

MISTAKE #1: Transferring Assets into Qualified Income Trusts.

[1] See Internal Revenue Manual, Part 21, Chapter 7, Section 13 on Assigning Employer Identification Numbers.

I have had consultations where clients have had Miller Trusts, prepared by other attorneys, who advised the individual to transfer bank account savings into the Income Trust (e.g. Medicaid applicant had $50,000.00 in a bank account and simply transferred it into a QIT account).

This is a prime example of an <u>inappropriate</u> use of a QIT.

Let the name be your guide: income trusts are for excess income ONLY.

There are some great strategies and tools we can discuss to protect assets for the purpose of becoming eligible for Florida long-term care Medicaid – but a Qualified Income Trust is not one of them!

MISTAKE #2: Allowing Qualified Income Trusts to accumulate too much value over time.

I have seen several instances of Medicaid recipients not understanding that they are supposed to spend the QIT funds on their health / medical / care needs – and as a result, the balance in the Miller Trust account starts to accumulate and regularly increase in value.

I try to emphasize that QIT accounts should come close to zeroing out every month.

First, by allowing QIT accounts to accumulate value, it is evident that those individuals are not using all resources available to them.

Secondly, QITs have a Medicaid-payback obligation after the Medicaid-recipient passes away – what a shame to needlessly have to pay money back to the government when that could have been avoided.

MISTAKE #3: Forgetting that the QIT needs to be Properly Funded Every Calendar Month and Income Can Change

Income-Only Trusts need to be properly used each and every calendar month, in which a Medicaid applicant/recipient's income exceeds the income cap. After a few months of being on Medicaid, some applicants (or their trustees) will occasionally think that the government no longer cares about the QIT and how it is used. This is a mistake: The Miller Trust needs to be properly funded every month the Medicaid recipient wants to continue receiving long-term care benefits.

In addition, a Medicaid recipient's income might change from time-to-time. A spouse might pass away (allowing the surviving spouse to receive their higher social security income or pension) or a Medicaid recipient might inherit an IRA from a deceased relative, resulting in new monthly distributions.

In any case where a Medicaid recipient's monthly income changes, this (a) needs to be properly reported to Medicaid; and (b) the correct adjustments to what is transferred into the Qualified Income Trust account needs to be calculated and made accordingly.

BIG TAKEAWAY

Qualified Income Trusts / Miller Trusts are required for Florida ICP Medicaid or Medicaid Waiver applicants who receive too much by way of income.

QITs are for excess income only and should not be used for those who have too much by way of countable assets.

All income, from all sources combined, which exceeds the income cap must be transferred into the QIT each and every calendar month.

CHAPTER 3.

MEDICAID ASSET TEST: NON-COUNTABLE ASSETS

Luckily, Medicaid does not require its recipients to be completely impoverished because certain assets will be deemed "exempt."

This means that Medicaid will not count certain assets against the applicant as part of the $2,000.00 Asset Cap.

HOUSE MAY BE EXEMPT FROM MEDICAID

If the Medicaid applicant is single: The house must be within the stated equity limits ($713,000 as of January 2024). If the Medicaid applicant either lives in the home or expresses an "intent to return home," the house is exempt.

As an example, if the Medicaid applicant's house is worth $800,000.00, but has a $100,000.00 mortgage, the homeowner only has $700,000.00 in equity which is below the equity limits stated above (i.e. the house is safe and not counted for Medicaid purposes). If the house is worth $800,000.00 with no mortgage, you and your Elder Care lawyer will need to explore other options for getting equity out of the house.

If married: when the healthy spouse (not receiving Medicaid benefits) continues to reside in the house, it is exempt, regardless of value (no equity limits) and not subject to Medicaid estate recovery.

This "unlimited value" exception to a primary residence also applies if there is a child under the age of 21 or a blind/disabled/special needs child living at home, regardless of age.

Adult Child Caregiver Exception.

If a Medicaid applicant's adult child has lived in the home for two years prior to their parent's admission to the nursing home, who can show that their presence delayed their parent's admission into a long-term care institution, then the parent can convey their house to the caregiver child for nominal value and it will be deemed a compensated transfer (not subject to the typical gifting-prohibition penalty).

Sibling Exception.

If a Medicaid applicant's sibling co-owns the home and resides there for at least one year prior to the Medicaid Recipient's admission to a nursing home, the institutionalized sibling can convey their portion of the home to the well sibling, and it will be deemed a compensated transfer (not subject to penalty).

OTHER NON-COUNTABLE ASSETS

- Income Producing Property - if it produces income consistent with fair market value.

- One car of any value. A second car 7 years old or older (and not deemed a luxury or classic/antique car).

- Irrevocable Pre-Paid Burial Arrangement (of any value) or up to $2,500.00 in a separate bank account designated for funeral/cremation/burial use.

- Burial expenses (grave sites, mausoleums, urns, caskets, headstones, etc.) for immediate family members of the Medicaid applicant.

- Personal property. Medicaid is generally not going to value your furniture, silverware, rugs, etc... unless there are items of unusual value (e.g. a Rembrandt painting hanging on your wall)

- Term Life Insurance Policies (with no cash value)

- Other Life insurance Policies - if the face value of all insurance policies combined is $2,500 or less (then the cash value is not counted).

- Qualified Retirement Accounts (such as an IRA, 401k, 403b, etc...) if it is paying out in regular or required minimum distributions per the applicant's life expectancy. While the value of the qualified account would not be counted as an asset, the distributions, however, would be counted as income and may necessitate the use of a Qualified Income Trust (further described in Chapter 2).

- Assets with multiple owners (if any are non-Medicaid recipients) because Medicaid cannot force a non-Medicaid recipient to sell an asset, they legally own. In this case, it is deemed "unavailable" to the Medicaid applicant and not counted against them. But, be warned: if the asset is sold, the Medicaid recipient must plan for what they will do with their portion of the proceeds (refusing or giving away their portion of net sale proceeds will result in a gift/disqualification period).

- Medicaid compliant annuities.

BIG TAKEAWAY

Not all assets count against the $2,000.00 asset limitation.

CHAPTER 4.

MEDICAID ASSET TEST: COUNTABLE ASSETS

Medicaid counts nearly everything not listed in Chapter 3 as an asset:

- Bank accounts/brokerage accounts (any bank or brokerage account with the Medicaid applicant's name on it is deemed accessible, and thus countable, to the Medicaid applicant);

- Any asset titled in the name of a revocable trust (revocable trusts do not serve a helpful role in Medicaid planning);

- Retirement accounts such as a 401(k) or IRA or Roth IRA (if not paying out in regular or required minimum distributions);

- Second homes or other non-homesteaded real estate (that are not being rented out for fair market value);

- Primary residence if equity exceeds current equity limit that changes every year and no other exception (described in Chapter 3) applies;

- Annuities (with a small exception of Medicaid-compliant annuities which very few people have unless they have been directed to obtain one by their Medicaid lawyer);

- Cash value of life insurance, if face value exceeds $2,500.00 (almost all non-term policies will have a face value that exceeds this amount);

- Second cars (if luxury, classic or late model);

- Pre-paid funeral plans (if not irrevocable).

Any asset in the name of the well/community spouse is deemed countable against the Medicaid applicant spouse (after subtracting the Community Spouse Resource Allowance, further described in Chapter 1).

A married couple is treated as one "unit" for Medicaid purposes.

WHAT HAPPENS WHEN A MEDICAID APPLICANT/RECIPIENT IS CO-OWNER ON A BANK OR BROKERAGE ACCOUNT?

I once met with a potential client in his 70s who lived with and took care of his blind and elderly mother (in her 90s). The client was on Medicaid, whereas his mother was not a Medicaid recipient. The son always had less than $2,000.00 in his bank account and needs his Medicaid for access to medical services that he would not otherwise be able to afford.

But the mother and son had a joint bank account so that it would be easier for the son to pay his mother's bills.

The Department of Children and Families (DCF) – the agency in Florida responsible for investigating whether someone is or is not eligible for Medicaid – found out about this and kicked him off Medicaid.

Why?

This is a well-intentioned mistake made all too frequently. The intention is usually for one person to simply pay bills for the other joint account holder - and, oftentimes, the joint owner who wants Medicaid has their own separate account and does not use the joint account for his or her own purposes.

The potential client was practically screaming, "I was just trying to help my blind mother live! The nurse needs to be paid, her electric bill needs to be paid, and she can't do it herself!!"

However, the Florida Medicaid ESS Manual explains (in Section 1640.0301) that when an individual joint account holder has unrestricted access to the funds in any account, Medicaid must presume all the funds in the account are owned by the individual (if two or more Medicaid recipients or applicants hold a joint account, Medicaid will divide and assign the funds equally).

So, regardless of the intentions of my potential client, he did not realize that DCF is required to presume that he had full access to the joint bank accounts with his mother.

However, DCF "must allow the [Medicaid recipient] to submit evidence to challenge this presumption."

Unfortunately, this may involve culling through years of bank statements to illustrate, to Medicaid's satisfaction, which withdrawals were used for the Medicaid recipient's purposes, and which were used to pay the non-Medicaid applicant's expenses.

As this can be a painfully laborious process, I recommend keeping separate accounts.

Instead of becoming a joint account holder, the Medicaid recipient should help the non-Medicaid recipient pay bills through a well-documented durable power of attorney.

In the above example, when Medicaid saw the son simply take his name off the account, they viewed that as his willingly giving up access to resources that were his. In the eyes of DCF, this is tantamount to gifting assets.

Giving assets away, within five years of applying to Medicaid or at any time while receiving Medicaid -- as we'll discuss below -- is the long-term care Medicaid program's cardinal sin.

GIFTING ASSETS AND THE FIVE-YEAR RULE

"Can't I just gift or give away assets before I apply to Medicaid?"

Unless you have five years until you are applying for Medicaid, the answer is generally: <u>NO!</u>

People get in trouble for this all the time. Here is the typical scenario:

An older adult wants Medicaid but has too many countable assets. He reads on the internet that he can only have $2,000.00 to his name.

The older adult does not meet with an experienced elder-law attorney and instead decides to just gift nearly all assets away to his grown children (after all, these are the people who are going to inherit anyway).

The problem is that Medicaid will impose a penalty period for the value of all gifts in the prior 60-month (five year) period.

This is often referred to as the "look-back period."

First, note that I use the terms "gift" and "transfer of assets" interchangeably. To be more precise, when I refer to gifting or a transfer of assets, I am talking about a situation in which a Medicaid recipient or Medicaid applicant gives something away without compensation or receiving fair-market value in return.

This is not to be confused with spending one's money, which is allowed.

For example, a Medicaid applicant can pay a contractor $25,000.00 to replace the roof of their home – that is not a gift or transfer of assets for less than fair-market value. Rather, this expense is, in fact, an example of a transfer of assets FOR fair-market value, which is perfectly acceptable to Medicaid/DCF and would not result in a penalty.

On the other hand, if a Medicaid applicant gives their child $25,000.00, that is an example of a gift or transfer of assets that will result in a transfer penalty.

Some people might try to be creative by asserting that they "paid" their child $25,000.00 to paint a room in their house. Medicaid will look at that as a "partial gift" - if the fair market value to paint a room in a house is $500.00, Medicaid would treat the transaction as a $24,500.00 gift, and assess a penalty accordingly.

Gift Penalty Exception: Spouses

Note, however, that spouses can gift to each other without limit or penalty. However, it is important to keep in mind that spouses are considered one "unit," so assets in either spouse's name are counted against the one spouse applying for or receiving Medicaid.

One example of why spouses might want to gift assets to each other is for a healthy spouse to take advantage of the Community Spouse Resources Allowance (CSRA) discussed in Chapter 1.

I should also mention that not all Medicaid programs assess a gift penalty. In Florida, for example, the QMB and Medically Needy Programs allow applicants to transfer assets without penalty.

We still don't recommend gifting, even if the Medicaid program allows, because we always consider the possibility of the same applicant requiring Medicaid Waiver or ICP long-term care services in the future.

How is the Medicaid Gifting Penalty Calculated?

Again, the most valuable of Medicaid programs, particularly Medicaid's long-term care programs, can and do assess a gifting penalty.

The Medicaid penalty period is calculated per a state formula. Add up all the gifts in the last five years and divide them by the Florida Medicaid Penalty Divisor (which is the average monthly cost of a nursing home in Florida). The result is the number of months that Medicaid will delay an approval.

The penalty period divisor as of January 2024 is: $10,438.00 (NOTE: this divisor changes periodically).

By way of example:

John wants to apply for Medicaid in February of 2024. John has a son and a daughter. After reviewing his financial records, the Medicaid caseworker notes that:

1. In July 2017, John transferred $104,380.00 to his brother;

2. In January 2020, John transferred his stock portfolio to his son (worth $104,380.00); and

3. In December 2021, because John loves his children equally, John also wrote his daughter a check for $104,380.

Besides these gifts, John is otherwise eligible for Medicaid.

The gift to his brother is beyond the 5-year Medicaid lookback period and so does not figure into the penalty period. However, the uncompensated transfers of funds to both of John's children are each within the five-year look back (if a Medicaid application is submitted in February 2024) and the Medicaid caseworker would add them up (together $208,760.00) and divide by the Medicaid penalty divisor: $216,180/$10,438.00 = 20.

As a result, Medicaid will refuse to pay for John's long-term care for a period of 20 months.

The penalty period starts from the date of the transfer or the date one applies to Medicaid and is otherwise eligible, whichever is later!

So, in our example, John will have to figure out how to privately pay for long-term care services he needs for the next one year and eight months!

The Medicaid penalty period has no cap. Therefore, if the gift is large enough, it is possible for the Medicaid penalty period to exceed five years.

When Does it Make Sense to Gift Assets Away?

Section 1640.0606 of the Florida ESS Policy Manual explains that the Transfer of Assets (or Income) Penalty applies to the Institutional Care Program (ICP), MEDS-AD, Institutionalized Hospice, Home and Community Based Service Programs (HCBS) (i.e. Medicaid Waiver that allows the recipient to live at home or in an ALF), and the Program for All-Inclusive Care for the Elderly (PACE), regardless of whether the Medicaid applicant is receiving SSI-Direct Assistance (cash) as well as non-SSI recipients.

Most clients who are seeking out an Elder Law Attorney are going to be applying (or planning to apply) to one of these programs.

Therefore, as stated above, an Elder Care Lawyer's initial response to the question of whether gifts are advisable, will almost always be a resounding "No!"

However, sometimes it makes sense to purposefully transfer or gift assets when contemplating applying for one of these programs. Most frequently this occurs when someone anticipates eventually needing home and community-based Medicaid or nursing-home Medicaid close to or after 5 years.

Perhaps someone is showing the first signs of dementia, or you or your loved one is in their 70s and in relatively good health. Or someone who is younger and knows that they have a family history of age-related dementia such as Alzheimer's or Parkinson's.

These are some common scenarios where it might make sense to meet with an Elder Care Attorney to discuss how to best protect their assets against the threat of long-term care expenses before actually needing any long-term care.

During our elder law consultation, we will talk about the 5-year Irrevocable Trust. This is sometimes referred to as a Medicaid Asset Protection Trust.

The 5-Year Irrevocable Medicaid Trust

In essence, the 5-Year Irrevocable Medicaid Trust involves intentionally gifting a substantial portion (not all) of your assets into a trust that you do not directly control. But you control who the trustees are, and retain the power to remove and replace them, if they act inappropriately. This Irrevocable Trust provides some other asset-protection benefits as well.

If, after 60 months, you need Medicaid, you can apply, and the assets owned by the 5-Year Medicaid Trust will be "invisible" and not subject to the transfer-of-assets penalty.

The irrevocable trust can hold bank/brokerage funds, real estate, cars, and nearly any other type of asset.

Income, earned by the irrevocable trust, can be distributable to the Medicaid applicant, the applicant's spouse, or the applicant's children. Different factors will be weighed, and discussed with your elder law attorney, regarding whether or not the Medicaid applicant should have the trust's income distributed to him/her.

Having access to the income might be good while receiving Medicaid at home or in an ALF. However, if an applicant moves to a nursing home, the irrevocable trust income (but not the trust's principal or assets) would have to go to the nursing home.

Importantly, principal can never be distributed to the applicant or the applicant's spouse. Principal distributions, during the applicant's life, can be made only to the children or other trusted loved ones listed as lifetime beneficiaries of the irrevocable trust. This is how and why the principal is not counted as an available asset to the applicant for Medicaid-eligibility purposes.

The future applicant and/or the spouse can keep money out of the trust to spend during the 5-year look-back period. Also, remember that the community spouse of the applicant, so long as he or she is not applying for Medicaid, can have up to the CSRA (refer to Chapter 1) on the day the applicant applies for Medicaid.

This means that money can still be held outside of the Irrevocable Trust and controlled by the applicant and/or spouse subject to when application is made.

Your Elder Law Attorney will guide you through the decision of how much to keep outside of the Irrevocable Medicaid asset protection trust.

The beneficiary (Medicaid applicant) will never have direct access or control over the assets placed into the irrevocable trust. Loss of control is, of course, the primary drawback to utilizing this strategy.

The irrevocable trust is often preferable to giving the assets away to a family member because the assets are safe (and creditor protected) in the irrevocable trust.

When one gives everything to a child, as opposed to an irrevocable trust, there are a whole host of potential risks involved. What if the child:

- gets divorced,
- goes bankrupt,
- has a gambling or addition problem,
- causes a car accident,
- what if they predecease you?

In short: if you gift assets directly to an individual, as opposed to an irrevocable trust, the assets are subject to that individual's creditors, alimony, misappropriation, and their individual estate plan.

There will always be a certain degree of risk involved when assets are placed directly into another individual's name. These risks can be mostly avoided by utilizing a well-drafted trust.

While we hope for the best, we also plan for the worst.

If Medicaid is needed within 60 months, we have backup strategies that will still allow my client to apply for Medicaid. Sometimes that involves private paying for long-term care for a period.

For example, if Medicaid is needed after 4 years and six months of transferring assets into the irrevocable trust, it might make sense to private pay for six months then apply for Medicaid. On the other hand, if my client needs to apply for Medicaid after only a year or two of transferring assets into an irrevocable trust, we might be forced to dissolve the trust and utilize another set of Medicaid-planning strategies.

THE MEDICAID 5-YEAR LOOK BACK PERIOD REVISITED

I wanted to directly address the Medicaid five year/60-month rule again, only because it is the cause of much confusion.

Many people are falsely under the impression that they cannot engage in Medicaid planning because, "I need long term care now and cannot wait five years." I hope this chapter has sufficiently debunked this widespread misinterpretation of the five-year rule.

Again, the 5-year rule does not mean that one cannot apply for or receive Medicaid benefits within five years or that they must wait five years after doing any sort of legal Medicaid planning.

The 5-year rule only restricts you or your loved one's access to Medicaid – if and only if – assets have been given away / gifted / transferred without receiving anything of fair-market value in return, within the past five years.

Period.

The gifting penalty can only be erased if the Medicaid recipient receives the value of the gift/transfer of assets back. In that case, the gift is deemed "cured."

As with much in life, timing is everything. So, if gifts were made 4 years and 10 months ago, it may make sense to wait two months before applying to Medicaid.

Otherwise, if the gift can be returned, or is not excessive, then it will make sense to meet with a Medicaid lawyer to discuss how to protect one's countable assets, which is the subject of the next chapter.

Most importantly: the Medicaid planning strategies we deploy when Medicaid is needed near term or now, in Florida, <u>do not trigger</u> or involve the Medicaid five-year lookback penalty.

Some of the strategies that can be utilized within five years (often within just a few months) of applying for Long-Term Care Medicaid in Florida are discussed in Chapter 5.

BIG TAKEAWAY

Most assets are countable (for Medicaid-eligibility determination purposes). The desire to protect these assets is generally the primary reason why someone sees an elder care lawyer who focuses on Medicaid planning.

Gifting should usually be avoided, unless you plan in advance (and even then, only done under the direction of an experienced elder law attorney).

Proper Medicaid Planning can legally and ethically be conducted within a few months of applying for Florida LTC Medicaid – you do not need to wait five years if assets are protected in a Medicaid-compliant manner. This is also sometimes referred to as the process of transforming assets from countable to non-countable.

CHAPTER 5.

How to Transform Countable Assets Into Non-Countable Assets

An Irrevocable Five-Year Medicaid trust may be the perfect solution for individuals who have the foresight to plan in advance - and can wait five years.

But most people seeking an Elder Law attorney desire Medicaid as soon as possible. In this situation, the 5-year irrevocable trust strategy won't work because it is intentionally gifting assets away (into the trust), which will impose the penalty period.

Most of my clients, who do not want to wait five years, own their home, and have between $50,000 and $650,000 in total countable assets – and they need Medicaid to help pay for home-health care, ALF care or skilled nursing facility care as soon as possible.

Luckily, we have other Medicaid-planning tools in our arsenal.

These tools allow us to convert countable assets into non-countable assets in a Medicaid-compliant way. In other words: a way that will not be judged as a gift by the Medicaid case examiner or a way that will not trigger the five-year look-back rule.

The following principles are based either around an applicable Federal law, or around the premise that a Medicaid applicant/recipient can spend their own money, which is why you may also refer to Medicaid planning strategies as part of a set of "spenddown" strategies.

All Medicaid spend down techniques have pros and cons, which I will briefly address here. Not all of these Medicaid-planning strategies will be appropriate for every case.

This is why it is essential to meet with a Medicaid-planning lawyer in person or over the phone (or increasingly Zoom/video) to discuss your unique set of circumstances in detail.

PERSONAL SERVICES CONTRACT

A personal services contract is also sometimes referred to as a "family caregiver agreement."

The Florida Supreme Court noted that Florida nursing-home law only requires nursing homes to provide slightly over two hours of actual care per resident per day – which means nursing home residents may spend most of the day without personal hands-on care.

If a Medicaid-applicant is residing in an ALF or at home, they are often reliant on family members or friends to assist with all sorts of tasks – from the mundane (e.g. paying bills) to the hands-on (e.g. making sure medicine is taken, assisting with cooking, bathing, ensuring that the Medicaid-applicant is receiving adequate care, etc...)

Some more examples include: attending care plan meetings at nursing home, interacting with lawyers, attending appointments with doctors, serving as an advocate, driving the elder to appointments or family gatherings, entertainment events, and more.

Enter the personal services contract.

Essentially, a personal services contract (or family caregiver agreement) is a contract between the Medicaid applicant and one or more designated caregivers for services that are not provided by the skilled nursing home, assisted living facility or at home.

The caregiver is usually a family member, such as an adult child, but it can be any adult with or without formal caregiving training or experience.

The payment for services under a personal service contract is based on the resident's life expectancy and can be made to the caregiver in a lump sum payment up front.

If the Medicaid applicant were to give $50,000 to their adult child, Medicaid would treat that transfer as a gift – and would impose a penalty (discussed in Chapter 4).

However, transferring $50,000 (if that amount is, as further described below, calculated to be of fair market value) as payment for caregiving services to be rendered pursuant to the terms of a personal services contract, then Florida Medicaid does not currently treat that transfer as a gift.

The personal services contract then becomes a useful tool to help the Medicaid applicant legally spend down their assets to help qualify for Medicaid in way that would not impose a penalty.

Courts have ruled that a properly drafted and fair personal services contract is not a gift and is completely appropriate.

Even though we expect our children to help us for free and out of love; the personal services contract recognizes the practical reality: being a care provider, even to a loved one, can be time-consuming and difficult. Caregiving is often a part-time, or even full-time, job.

There is no legal requirement that anyone (family member or not) provide these caregiving services for free. In fact, this very issue was challenged, and ruled upon (in favor of using the family caregiver agreement) by the 4th District Court of Appeal in Florida.[2]

What is a Fair Rate to Pay on a Personal Services Contract?

Like everything else in the Medicaid-planning world – payments made to any third party (including family), in return for items or services, must be made at fair-market value. If a payment is made for less than fair-market value, we risk triggering the five-year lookback gift penalty.

Here is the formula:

- Fair Market Value on a Personal Services Contract = a fair hourly rate x estimated hours per week x 52 (the number of weeks in a year) x life expectancy in years.

It is important to establish a fair hourly rate within the bounds of what Florida Medicaid deems reasonable, which is why this is not a DIY project, an experienced elder care attorney is essential.

A professional geriatric care manager (who can be employed as part of a Medicaid qualification strategy, if there is no trusted family member or friend willing, able, or available to assist) might charge between $75.00 to $130.00 per hour. For a non-professional family member such as an adult child (who is not a nurse, geriatric care manager, social worker, medical professional, etc...).

Our firm uses a highly discounted rate (because the family member is usually not a certified geriatric care manager and many services provided likely do not fall within the purview of a

---

[2] *Thomas v. Dept of Children*, 707 So 2d 954 (Fla. 4th DCA 1998).

geriatric care manager anyway, e.g. help with ADLs would more affordably be provided by a Certified Nursing Assistant – CNA).

Professional bill-paying services, hiring someone to drive your love one to doctors appointments, to the store, etc... can be purchased at a significantly lower rate as well.

The caregiver will be asked to keep time sheets to show that the hours contemplated in the family caregiver agreement / personal services contract are real and to justify money received.

Life expectancy is calculated using the Medicaid's life expectancy actuarial tables. For Medicaid planning purposes, the earlier a personal-services contract is signed, the better, because the earlier the individual needs the services, the more money we can justify transferring under the terms of the family caregiver agreement.

Why Sign a Personal Services Contract Before Medicaid is Needed?

Life expectancy creates the major financial limitation when utilizing a personal services contract as part of a Medicaid-planning or Medicaid-qualification strategy.

- The older someone is, the lower their life expectancy.

- The lower their life expectancy, the less money can be transferred to the caregiver.

- The less money that can be transferred, penalty-free, to a caregiver, the more we need to rely upon other Medicaid strategies that may not allow for as much money to stay in the family. This effect itself is not inherently bad or evil, sometimes the personal services contract is, in fact, not in line with the Medicaid-applicant's goals or needs.

There is no need to wait until an elder is immediately sick (and long-term care costs are imminent) to enter into a personal services contract (although we elder law attorneys often have to work on this basis). Signing a personal services contract as part of pre-planning (instead of crisis planning), allows the pre-planner to lock in that higher life-expectancy rate if there is work that needs to be performed even before Medicaid would be desired.

This allows more assets to be transferred out of the Medicaid applicant's name when the time comes to qualify and apply for Medicaid.

The personal services contract is drafted to be payable on demand, so no actual money needs to change hands immediately.

Money can be transferred to the service provider the month or day before the elder applies for Medicaid – even if the personal services contract was initially signed months or years prior.

Benefits of a Medicaid Personal Services Contract

- Receive care from a trusted family member or friend, without becoming a financial burden on them.

- Assists in getting assets out of applicant's name, without penalty (if properly drafted and documented), to help qualify for Medicaid to pay for additional home health care, assisted living facility care or nursing home care.

- A form of estate planning: Ideally, a personal services contract involves giving money to someone who would have inherited it as a beneficiary under a Last Will & Testament or Revocable Trust anyway (but this is not always the case).

- Usually, Medicaid applicants want to keep the money in the family instead of going to pay for the nursing home or government. This benefits the Medicaid recipient because now, their adult child (or other caregiver) has plenty of money to provide for themselves and, if they choose, assist with the Medicaid recipient's other care expenses. However, the contract cannot provide that the money be restricted for any purpose - this is one of the risks described below.

- While preferable, the caregiver does not necessarily need to live locally. There are books written about long-distance caregiving. Certainly, tasks such as paying bills, reviewing health care documentation, dealing with the lawyer, checking in on loved ones, keeping the rest of the family informed and more are examples of services that can be done from afar.

Personal Service Contract Restrictions and Risks

The personal services contract is "executory," meaning the caregiving services are to be provided "as needed" even if payment is not made until later.

The services provided must not duplicate services already being provided by the assisted living facility or nursing home. Also, the Medicaid caregiver agreement must be prospective, not retroactive (much to the dismay of many adult children of clients I work with, who have been providing significant services to their elderly parent for years, a caregiver cannot be paid for services previously provided or performed).

Once the contract amount is "called in" by the caregiver, it cannot be refunded or returned (or Medicaid would count it as a resource available to the applicant)

- Because personal service contracts are non-refundable, the most worrisome major risk of transferring money to a caregiver, in one lump sum, is losing control of the asset. What if the caregiver takes the money and moves to Fiji? Or goes to Vegas and puts it all on red? Or gets divorced? Or gets sued? Or declares bankruptcy? Therefore, it is important to enter into a personal services caregiving agreement only with someone you trust completely.

- o If this is a concern, sometimes we utilize a device called a Third-Party Special Needs Trust (which is much different from the other types of trusts discussed in this book) to protect funds transferred via a Personal Services Contract.

- A personal-services contract may create inconsistencies with an existing estate plan. For example: if three children were supposed to inherit money equally, but now one local child (the designated caregiver under the personal services caregiver contract) gets a lump sum in advance, this could be perceived as unfair to the other two children.

- Finally, the IRS will likely treat this transfer of money as a taxable event for the caregiver who receives the money (i.e. it is taxable income to the caregiver). I am not a tax lawyer or CPA and will always advise our clients and their care provider (under a personal services contract) to seek the advice of a qualified tax professional. There may be ways to diffuse / defer the tax burden on the caregiver that are beyond the scope of this book. Again, I always defer to tax professionals and always advise my clients to speak to someone qualified to give tax advice about this matter.

JOINTLY OWNED ASSETS

The Department of Children and Families (the agency that administers Florida's Medicaid programs) takes the position that any individual who has the legal ability to unilaterally dispose of an asset is considered an owner of the asset. That asset, in turn, is deemed available to the person and thus is a countable resource.

But what happens when an asset has more than one owner?

In Chapter 4, we discussed the problem with shared bank accounts (if your name is on the account, you can, technically, withdraw 100% of the money, so the entire account is deemed available to you). However, some assets with multiple owners are not 100% accessible by any one owner.

An example: the vacation home that has been in the family for generations. Grandma and grandpa may have originally owned that lake house, but when they passed away, it was inherited by their three children. Let us suppose that the three children have grown older and now, only one of those children is applying for Medicaid. Let's further suppose that the lake house is worth $5,000,000.00.

The lake house, a five-million-dollar asset, is completely non-countable for Medicaid-eligibility purposes.

Why?

The reason is: the Medicaid applicant cannot force his siblings to sell the lake house. Medicaid has no jurisdiction over non-Medicaid recipients. So, the value or the equity in the lake house is deemed not available to the Medicaid applicant. As a result, Medicaid will not count this jointly-owned asset against the Medicaid applicant.

The above example supposes that an asset started as jointly owned. But as a Medicaid-planning strategy, a Medicaid applicant is free to purchase assets with other non-Medicaid eligible owners. There are several times when this makes complete sense.

If a Medicaid applicant is living in their child's home, as plenty of senior citizens do as they age, the Medicaid applicant could consider purchasing an equity interest in their child's home. If the house is worth $300,000.00 and the Medicaid applicant has an extra $100,000.00 that they need to spend down, they could purchase a 1/3rd interest in their child's house. This would be a bona fide real estate transaction, with closing costs, a new deed recorded, etc.

In this example, there is no gift: The Medicaid applicant is purchasing an equity interest in the place where they are living. A fair transaction.

This arrangement has the side benefit of removing an asset from the probate process. After the Medicaid applicant passes away, title will automatically vest in the child (assuming the joint ownership is titled properly).

Maybe mom or dad doesn't want to move in with their child. There's no reason why they can't go in on a deal together - e.g. become joint investors in a business, or a piece of rental real estate.

If everything is done at fair-market value - joint ownership of assets, if not abused and done correctly under the supervision of an experienced elder care lawyer, can be a great Medicaid-planning technique.

Risks and Drawbacks to Jointly-Owned Property

The risk, however remote, is what happens if the non-Medicaid owners pass away before the Medicaid recipient?

In our example above, this would mean that title would revert back to the Medicaid recipient, which would become a countable asset jeopardizing Medicaid eligibility and thus require him/her to rush and make other arrangements.

Another example is: what if a jointly-owned asset needs to be sold?

If an asset needs to be sold, all owners need to receive their fair portion of the proceeds (the Medicaid applicant cannot simply refuse to accept what they are owed after an asset is sold - as it will be treated as a gift and result in a disqualification penalty period).

As with any sudden influx of resources, the Medicaid applicant has about 30 days, after the excess assets are received, to engage in the proper planning techniques to remain or become Medicaid eligible. Therefore, speaking with an elder care lawyer, in advance, is important and necessary.

There are, of course, tax implications with any large asset purchase or sale. Again, I defer to your tax professional to properly advise you on all tax-related matters.

In addition, we have seen DCF/Medicaid call a transaction abusive when a Medicaid applicant, shortly before applying, buys an asset with someone in a way that doesn't make sense. One example is a nursing home resident (without any chance of leaving the facility) purchasing an equity interest in their child's home who lives out of state. There is no realistic ability, in this example, for the Medicaid recipient to utilize the asset and can be deemed and abuse of the system. So, this strategy should only be used in appropriate / situation-specific contexts.

RENTAL REAL ESTATE

Pursuant to Medicaid rules, any real estate owned by the applicant that is being rented to a separate entity (including family or friends, so long as rents are at a rate within community standards) is not counted as an available asset to the applicant.

In other words, if the applicant purchases a home, or a second home, and rents it to another individual, the asset/funds used to purchase the home would no longer be a countable asset against the applicant, as those assets are invested in a form that is deemed "not available" or "non-countable."

Specifically, Section 1640.0544 of the ESS Policy Manual (also commonly referred to as the Florida Medicaid Manual) says that the fair market value of any income-producing property can be excluded by Medicaid as a countable resource (i.e. deemed exempt), even if used only on a seasonal basis (such as vacation homes).

But Florida Medicaid Won't Let You Charge Unreasonably Cheap Rent

This strategy will NOT allow the Medicaid applicant to purchase a second home and rent it out to their child for some unreasonably low number, such as $10.00 per month.

Again, the law requires the rent to be within community standards for similar homes (i.e. fair market value rents only).

How Does Rent Impact the Medicaid Income Test?

While the rental-producing property Medicaid strategy solves an asset problem (i.e. it allows you convert countable resources into non-countable resources), it creates additional income.

As we discussed in Chapter 2, Medicaid has an income cap limit. Medicaid will add up the income from all sources (social security, pension, 401k, etc.). This will now include your newly acquired rental income.

If the income, from all sources, exceeds the threshold (also called the income test or income cap), a QIT (qualified income trust / miller trust) will be necessary.

In addition, a portion of the rental income may be added to the Medicaid recipient's "patient responsibility" calculation if they are in a nursing home. However, thankfully:

Florida Medicaid Lets You Deduct Certain Ordinary and Allowable Expenses from the Rental Income Calculation

It is important that these allowable deductions be presented properly in the Florida Medicaid application in the form of a Medicaid-Compliant Budget, along with a Medicaid-Compliant Property Management Agreement.

Section 1840.0504 of the Florida Medicaid manual explains that ordinary and necessary expenses that can be deducted from rental income include:

- Real estate taxes
- Interest on debts (mortgage principal cannot be deducted)
- Utilities
- Maintenance
- Repairs (i.e. minor corrections to existing structure)
- Cost of advertising for renters
- Lawn service
- Interest and escrow
- Homeowner's Insurance

Property Management Fee as another Necessary and Ordinary Expense from Medicaid Income Calculation

Interestingly, Medicaid rules also allow an amount of up to 10% of the rental income to be deducted for "management expenses." "Management" can be anyone, including a family member without a property manager's license, who the applicant assigns by contractual agreement to manage the property.

Using income-producing property or purchasing rental property is a great way to shelter significant assets, produce extra income (which benefits the Medicaid recipient who lives at home or in an ALF, but will result in a higher "patient responsibility" amount if in a nursing home), and provides some measure of an estate that can benefit the Medicaid recipient's heirs after the person receiving Medicaid passes away.

Risks and Drawbacks to Rental/Income Producing Property

However, like all Medicaid-planning techniques, this strategy has its drawbacks:

Someone must actively manage the property, there is the risk of having a bad tenant that damages the property or requires eviction, and, of course, a closing may be required which will require the payment of closing costs and recording fees and may be a lengthy process.

While the additional income stream can really improve the quality of life for someone in an ALF or living at home, that income stream is subject to being cut off with a bad tenant or if the property goes through a period of being vacant.

Also, if the Medicaid recipient requires nursing home care, the nursing home will receive the additional income (but since the asset is protected, and with proper planning, can be designed to avoid Medicaid Estate Recovery -- this may be an acceptable drawback).

SPOUSAL REFUSAL

Spousal Refusal is also known as "Just Say No." It is available in Florida, but not every other state.

To start: if both spouses want Medicaid, "spousal refusal" is not an option.

In addition, if the Medicaid-applicant is not in a skilled nursing, rehab or long-term care facility setting (i.e. applying for institutional care placement Medicaid) there is some argument in the Florida elder law community as to whether "spousal refusal" is a valid option.

This Medicaid strategy works best when: the Medicaid applicant is living in a skilled nursing/LTC facility, while the other community spouse remains at home and is unlikely to require Medicaid in the near future.

There are two pillars that form the foundation of this "Just-Say-No" Medicaid-planning tool:

(1) The first pillar is based on the fact that intra-spousal transfers are not considered gifts. So, one spouse may, at any time and for any reason, transfer assets to the other spouse and the transfer will not be subject to a transfer penalty.

Remember that this is the gifting exception, not the rule. If one were to gift/transfer assets to anyone but their spouse, without receiving fair-market value in return, within five years, there would be a penalty).

In a Medicaid planning context, then, the spouse who is applying for Medicaid can transfer the bulk of their assets (all but $2,000.00) to the community spouse alone.

(2) The second pillar of "Just Say No" is that the Florida Supreme Court has held that spouses are not required to support one another. That is, one spouse is not responsible to pay the debts or obligations that solely belong to the other spouse.

The Florida ESS Manual provides that the community spouse can indicate their refusal to make assets available to the other spouse that needs Medicaid by signing a Notice of Spousal Refusal of Support.

However, the Department of Children and Families will require that the Medicaid applicant sign an Assignment of Rights to Support to the State of Florida.

There are some drawbacks to this strategy.

SPOUSAL REFUSAL RISKS AND DRAWBACKS

Loss of Income Diversion

With spousal refusal / just say no, there is an element of, "you can't have your cake and eat it too."

The first drawback to "Just Say No," is that the community spouse would forego his or her income allowance (i.e. MMMNA, discussed in Chapter 1). DCF takes the very reasonable position that if the community spouse is going to refuse to support the institutionalized spouse, then the community spouse forfeits the benefit of their income allowance.

Risk of Department of Children and Families (DCF) Taking Action

Recall the last step in "Spousal Refusal" is for the Medicaid beneficiary to assign their rights to demand support to the State. The reason is based on Florida Statute, §61.09 related to dissolution of marriages, which provides that if someone has the financial wherewithal to support their spouse (or minor child) but fails to do so, the spouse who is not receiving support can seek alimony without seeking a divorce.

With the assignment of support rights, the Medicaid spouse is assigning to the State of Florida their right to seek alimony outside of the context of divorce - up to the amount Medicaid is paying.

But, as discussed above, the Florida Supreme Court has held that spouses are not required to support one another.

Elder Law lawyers who handle Medicaid planning agree that there is very little likelihood of DCF being successful in trying to bring such a suit. To date, I have never heard of the State ever attempting such a maneuver.

The risk is apparently minimal. But we cannot account for a potential future change in policy and priorities by our state agencies.

If you like the "spousal refusal" concept, but want to ensure there is never a risk of lawsuit by the State of Florida, we occasionally guide our married clients (with the help of outside counsel) through a "strategic divorce." You can remain married in the eyes of your family, religion, and each other, but – after transferring assets while married, obtain a legal divorce in the eyes of the State.

SPENDDOWN ON ITEMS ACTUALLY NEEDED OR WANTED

This "Medicaid planning" technique should probably be the first one mentioned.

Never forget that Medicaid applicants can spend their money on anything that they desire or need. Even before any of the above Medicaid-planning techniques are discussed, I like to talk about what the person desiring Medicaid might practically need, want, or benefit from.

Practical Spend Down Items

Some practical ways to spend a Medicaid applicant's money might include: paying off the mortgage, making improvements to the home, paying off credit card debt, trading in to get a nicer and safer vehicle, or pre-paying for funeral and burial expenses.

If an irrevocable funeral plan is purchased, the entire amount is considered non-countable, and does much to ease the burden on family members after their loved one has passed away. It is an expense that will be incurred eventually, so might as well take care of it now. While not frequently utilized, a Medicaid applicant is also able to prepay for the funeral expenses of the entire immediate family.

Other practical considerations may include paying for needed repairs around the home.

Need a new roof or new kitchen? Go for it.

Don't actually "need" a new kitchen, but simply "want" a modernized upgrade? Wants are just as allowable as needs.

AC unit on its last legs? Replace it before it breaks down in the middle of summer!

If the home or vehicle needs to be made more handicap accessible, especially if the Medicaid applicant is still in the home, now is the time to incur those expenses. These expenses have the side benefit of increasing the value of these already exempt assets.

Enjoy Life Spend Down Items

After the necessities have been taken care of, I like to ask my clients: think about what will make your life better? What little luxuries might make my client's days more enjoyable?

Before applying for Medicaid, it would be fine for my client to purchase and mount a big screen TV in their room if they love certain programs or movies.

They can hire a music therapist or install a nice sound system if they enjoy music.

There are cruises that specifically cater to elderly and disabled individuals – even those with dementia and Alzheimer's.

They need not only spend their money on practical necessities (although, obviously those should be taken care of first) - purchasing items that add to their comfort or enjoyment are also allowed.

These Medicaid spend down items and services discussed obviously are not a comprehensive list.

So long as the Medicaid applicant is paying fair-market value for the service or product that they use (read: cannot buy gifts for others) Medicaid should not have a problem with it.

The only caveat is: don't get greedy with the personal items. Luxury items can be counted. Purchasing any item of extraordinary value, (e.g. an original Picasso or Cartier diamond necklace or Ferrari) won't help anyone qualify for Medicaid.

COUNTABLE ASSETS → NON-COUNTABLE ASSETS CONCLUSION

Again, in an attempt to keep this book relatively short and easy-to-read, the Medicaid asset protection strategies are not all listed or comprehensively discussed. For example, there are Irrevocable Medicaid Annuity products that are rarely used, but very useful in certain situations.

There are real estate investment funds and special promissory note strategies, which will assist in qualifying for Medicaid.

Annuities, Real Estate Investments, Notes and other Medicaid-planning techniques are more appropriate to discuss with your local experienced Elder Law attorney if appropriate to your situation - as opposed to in this book.

The next chapter discusses Special Needs Trusts, which are another way to spend down assets.

Because they are complex legal structures, a separate chapter is dedicated to them.

CHAPTER 6.

SPECIAL NEEDS TRUST

A special needs trust (sometimes called a "supplemental needs trust") is a specialized trust that is specifically designed to hold assets in a way that allows the beneficiary to preserve or obtain need-based public benefits such as SSI or Medicaid.

The assets in a special needs trust are managed by a private or professional trustee and used to maintain and increase the beneficiary's quality of life by purchasing products or services that are not covered by the public benefit.

To complicate things further, there are a variety of different types of special needs trusts.

The types of Special Needs Trusts discussed in this chapter should not be confused with the Irrevocable Five-Year Trusts discussed in Chapter 4. They are also very different from the more popular and widely known Revocable Living Trusts used in estate planning.

Assets placed into a properly drafted and executed special-needs trust (SNT) are 100% non-countable for Medicaid and SSI eligibility. Furthermore, an unlimited amount of assets may be placed in a special-needs trust.

Assets can be placed into a properly-drafted SNT at any time (no need to wait 5 years), and the transfer will not result in a penalty per federal law.

Below are a few common examples of when it may make sense to utilize a special needs trust:

A Parent with Disabled Child Does Not Want to Disinherit Their Child, But Doesn't Want to Jeopardize the Child's Medicaid Benefits Either

In this situation, the parent's elder law attorney would suggest the creation of a testamentary third party special needs trust for the benefit of their disabled child. This would be a trust created out of the parent's Will or created as a subtrust (i.e. a trust-within-a-trust) within their existing Revocable Living Trust.

Upon the death of the parent, a special needs trust would be created, and managed by a trustee who would provide only for items and services not covered by Medicaid.

Because testamentary special needs trusts are also considered third party special needs trusts (i.e. created from the assets of someone other than the beneficiary), there is no Medicaid payback requirement.

Sometimes Third-Party Special Needs Trusts are created as a stand-alone trust so that others can contribute to the well-being of a special-needs individual (of any age) without jeopardizing their access to SSI or Medicaid.

Spousal Testamentary Special Needs Trusts

We also see a similar situation in which a sick spouse requires nursing home care. The well spouse doesn't want to disinherit the sick spouse but doesn't want to jeopardize the nursing home spouse's Medicaid approval if the well spouse dies first.

Again, if the well spouse predeceases the Medicaid applicant, the well spouse's assets would (if proper planning was completed in advance, likely by an experienced elder-law attorney) go into a special needs trust created out of their Last Will & Testament, for the sole benefit of the Medicaid recipient. This would have the effect of protecting the Medicaid recipient's public benefits without a Medicaid payback requirement.

Medicaid Compliant First Party Special Needs Trusts

The Federal Code that addresses the types of Medicaid Compliant <u>Special Needs Trusts</u> (SNT) can be found at 42 USC 1396(p)(d)(4)(A) and (d)(4)(C).

I cite this particular code (whereas other citations are scant in this book) because Self Settled Special Needs Trusts and Pooled Special Needs Trusts (both are examples of Medicaid compliant, First-Party Special Needs Trusts) are also sometimes referred to by the last three subheadings of the code in which they are addressed.

For example, Self-Settled SNTs are sometimes called "d4A Trusts," and Pooled SNTs are sometimes referred to as "d4C Trusts."

Assets placed in either a Self-Settled or a Pooled SNT will not be counted as an asset for Medicaid-qualification purposes. Also, the process of transferring assets into a Medicaid compliant SNT will not be deemed a gift or transfer subject to a penalty.

The trustee(s) of an SNT can use the funds placed into the trust to purchase items and services not already provided by Medicaid, including but not limited to: housekeeping, cooking, home decor, computers, televisions, appliances, grooming, salon services, dry cleaning, entertainment, recreation, transportation costs, educational needs or supplies, music lessons, musical instruments, linens, towels, bedding, yard services, home security, attorneys, coaches, accountants, and more.

Beware: There are certain items (that will be counted as "unearned income" or "in kind support and maintenance") that will result in a reduction in SSI benefits and may potentially result in a temporary or full loss of Medicaid, which are beyond the scope of this book and why it is incredibly important to seek the guidance of an Elder care lawyer who regularly handles Medicaid planning and drafts special needs trusts.

Self-Settled Special Needs Trusts

The "grantor" or "settlor" is the legal lingo used to describe the person who creates any type of trust. Therefore a "Self-Settled" SNT is a SNT created with assets of a person with a disability who is also to be the beneficiary. Sometimes these trusts are called First Party SNTs for the same reason.

Contrast this with a "Third Party SNT" which is created out of assets of a third party (someone other than the beneficiary).

First rule of Self-Settled SNTs: if the beneficiary is 65 or older, they are not able to utilize this tool.

Do not pass go. Do not collect $200. Stop reading and seek another type of trust or Medicaid qualification strategy.

The major characteristics of a First Party/d4A SNT are:

- The SNT must be irrevocable.

- The beneficiary's assets are what is placed into the trust.

- The beneficiary may not also be the trustee.

- The SNT must contain a Medicaid-payback provision (discussed below)

- Again, it's worth repeating, the beneficiary must be under age 65 when their assets are placed inside this SNT.

Pooled Special Needs Trusts

Pooled/d4C SNTs are useful for several reasons. The first is, there is no age requirement. The Medicaid applicant/recipient can be over the age of 65 and still utilize a pooled special needs trust.

Second, not everyone has a trustee that they can literally "trust," which is why someone under the age of 65 might be interested in a pooled special needs trust as well.

A pooled SNT, by definition, involves placing assets with a not-for-profit institution, so the funds are professionally managed (fee is typically between 1.5% - 3.5% per year).

A pooled SNT can be a first party SNT, third party SNT, or a combination thereof. A pooled SNT might start with assets of the beneficiary, but over time, friends and family are free to contribute assets as well into a separate trust account. You would want to separate the funds because "first party" funds are subject to Medicaid estate recovery, while "third party" funds are not.

Otherwise, the restrictions are the same as a First Party SNT. Money in the SNT can only be spent on items or services not already covered by Medicaid.

Another reason to utilize a Pooled SNT is to have the benefit of working with a professional. Using a family member to be a First Party SNT trustee sounds good in theory, but they have a tremendous responsibility. Failing to abide by the SNT's terms and conditions could jeopardize the Medicaid recipient's benefits. It also has other administrative obligations, such as: filing tax returns and periodic reporting to Medicaid.

A professional trustee handles the administration and is significantly less likely to make a distribution that would put the beneficiary's public benefits at risk.

The pooled special needs trust money is usually very conservatively invested and may earn more than the stated administrative fee.

Warning: Pooled Special Needs Trusts may not be advisable, or require additional restrictions, for those who receive both Social

Security Income (SSI, which is different and can be confused with Social Security Retirement) and are over the age of 65.

Again, this is very much not a "do-it-yourself" project. It is always important to seek the advice of an experienced elder law attorney before engaging in Medicaid planning.

Medicaid Compliant Special Needs Trusts - the Payback Provision

Both First Party and Pooled SNTs share a major drawback: the Medicaid payback provision.

If there are any assets remaining in either trust when the Medicaid beneficiary passes away, the trustee MUST notify Medicaid.

Medicaid will provide a lien up to the amount they have paid out if the beneficiary is over the age of 55. All funds remaining in the SNT must go toward satisfying this lien before it may pay out to any intended family members/heirs.

However, if there are no funds remaining in the SNT, then there is nothing to payback. This is why SNTs are often tools used in conjunction with other Medicaid-planning strategies.

This is also why parents, relatives, or friends, who are interested in helping out a Medicaid-recipient (by contributing assets or funds), should meet with an elder law attorney to create a third-party special needs trust that does not have a Medicaid payback obligation.

CHAPTER 7.

PROTECTING MEDICAID ELIGIBILITY AFTER A PERSONAL INJURY SETTLEMENT OR RECEIVING AN INHERITANCE.

The focus of this book, thus far, has been with an eye toward assisting those who have too much by way of assets or income. We have discussed some of the strategies used to legally and ethically shelter those assets to become Medicaid eligible.

However, elder law/Medicaid planning lawyers also assist those who already have Medicaid and receive a sudden influx of resources.

Primarily, I see this happen when a Medicaid recipient receives an inheritance or when the Medicaid recipient receives proceeds from a personal-injury or medical-malpractice settlement. But the principles in this chapter apply to most any other way someone might come into money, such as the division of assets because of a divorce settlement (know a Medicaid recipient whose office lottery pool just hit the winning numbers? Refer them to this book!).

We have already discussed how Medicaid recipients must constantly maintain assets below $2,000.00. If their assets ever exceed $2,000.00 throughout any calendar month, they will no longer be Medicaid eligible (one must have less than $2,000.00 at least one day during each calendar month).

So, when someone receives a lump-sum inheritance, injury settlement, or sells an exempt asset: receipt of those funds can be bittersweet.

THE MEDICAID RECIPIENT HAS TWO OPTIONS:

(1) VOLUNTARILY GIVE UP THEIR MEDICAID; OR (2) TAKE ACTION TO PRESERVE THEIR MEDICAID.

Dropping Medicaid After Receiving New Resources/Assets

If a Medicaid recipient is going to receive significant personal-injury-case proceeds or inheritance, they may find themselves in a financial position where they can well afford to privately pay for their own health insurance or may no longer need their food stamps, LTC or SSI assistance. Excellent! You are always free to voluntarily leave any needs-based public benefits program.

However, you should still inform the Social Security Administration and/or the Department of Children and Families that there has been a "change in circumstances."

You want to voluntarily notify DCF/SSA that you no longer wish to receive benefits because, if you fail to report that you are no longer eligible and unwittingly continue to receive benefits when no longer eligible, Medicaid / SSA will eventually find out. When they do, government agencies may send you a bill demanding to be reimbursed for funds that Medicaid should not have paid during the month's eligibility was lost.

Keeping Medicaid After Receiving New Resources / Assets

Much more often than not, a Medicaid recipient will come into funds (via inheritance, personal injury settlement, or sale of an asset) that does not result in them suddenly being independently wealthy. While coming into money is always nice, it doesn't mean you want to lose public benefits such as SSI or Medicaid.

These people must take action in the same calendar month when funds are available to a Medicaid beneficiary.

It is actually best to have your benefits-preservation plan in place well before the funds are received!

The timing of this is very important (which is why it makes sense for you to talk to a Medicaid-planning lawyer ASAP when you know an influx of funds are coming in soon).

Florida Medicaid alone gives you some extra time because you need to have less than $2,000.00 at least one day each calendar month.

But if you have Florida Medicaid in conjunction with the needs-based SSI program (again, not to be confused with social security retirement) you have to have less than $2,000.00 on the first day of each calendar month.

In other words, if you have both SSI and Medicaid and receive funds on January 2nd, you have the luxury of being able to figure out how to remain Medicaid and SSI eligible for the rest of January.

On the other hand, receiving new assets on January 28th will require a rush to figure out how to preserve SSI/Medicaid eligibility before February 1st.

See Chapter 5 and 6 for some methods Florida Medicaid lawyers use to remain Medicaid eligible after receiving an influx of assets.

Important: not all strategies that work for Medicaid alone will also work for those who have SSI and Medicaid.

No Gifting! | Don't Give Away Assets and Expect to Remain Medicaid Eligible.

The biggest mistake you can make after receiving personal injury proceeds or an inheritance is giving any portion of it away.

Gifts, as further discussed in Chapter 4, result in Medicaid ineligibility penalty periods.

I should reemphasize here, often Medicaid recipients think that because the IRS allows gifts of up to $17,000 (as of January 2024) that giving an amount less than that will allow them to retain their Medicaid.

It will not.

This line of thinking often gets those who want Medicaid into trouble. Medicaid gifting rules are completely different and separate from IRS gifting rules.

BIG TAKEAWAY

Someone on needs-based government benefits will rarely have an excuse if they fail to plan in advance. This is because coming into money is rarely a surprise:

Personal injury settlements can take months or years to come to fruition.

Inheritances may have to go through a probate process before funds are available to you.

If you need to sell an exempt asset, such as a house, you can choose a closing date.

It is important to meet with a Medicaid Planning/Elder Law attorney well in advance of coming into money if you want to protect your Medicaid (and/or SSI) benefits.

CHAPTER 8.

MEDICAID ESTATE RECOVERY

Florida Statutes, Chapter 409[3] is known as the "Medicaid Estate Recovery Act." It derives its authority from the Omnibus Budget Reconciliation Act of 1993 (known as OBRA-93) which mandated that all states, including Florida, seek recovery from the estate of a Medicaid recipient.

In other words, Medicaid recovery allows the Medicaid agency to file a claim against the estate of a Medicaid recipient.

Essentially, it creates a debt that only must be paid upon the death of the Medicaid recipient, from the probatable estate. When an estate is probated in Florida, Medicaid is a Class 3 general creditor[4].

Medicaid's right to estate recovery is limited to the value of medical / long-term care services provided to the Medicaid recipient.

If there are no cash assets available to satisfy the Medicaid estate recovery claim, Medicaid may force the sale of non-exempt personal property or real property (not homestead) if the costs of sale do not exceed the expected proceeds.

---

[3] See Florida Statutes, §409.9101
[4] See Florida Statutes, §733.707

Note that states differ in the types of assets they can seek, and the collections lengths they will go through to recoup available assets under Medicaid Estate Recovery.

EXCEPTIONS AND LIMITATIONS TO MEDICAID ESTATE RECOVERY

- Generally, Medicaid does not engage in its recovery effort until the Medicaid recipient passes away (an exception to this is in the case of a personal-injury recovery).

- If Medicaid pays benefits to someone who is under age 55, no debt is created.

- Medicaid will not enforce its debt in probate if, when the Medicaid recipient dies, he/she is survived by a spouse, child under the age of 21, a child who is deemed permanently disabled by social security standards, or a child who is blind.

- Medicaid cannot recover from property that is exempt from creditors (e.g. homestead property).

- Medicaid cannot recover from an estate under probate if the Medicaid estate recovery would result in an undue hardship for qualified heirs.

In Florida, Medicaid can only recover from the probate estate.

The significance of this is huge.

Florida's Medicaid estate recovery standards are why it is incredibly important to engage in proper estate planning and proper Medicaid planning (an elder law attorney does both).

Assets in a revocable living trust can be accessed by creditors if there are insufficient assets to cover debts in the deceased's estate.

However, with proper Medicaid planning by an experienced elder law attorney, the bulk of the Medicaid recipient's assets will be sheltered and pass outside of probate.

The one asset that most of my clients fear losing to Medicaid is their home.

Is my house at risk?

It could be. But as described above, Medicaid will not assert its recovery against a homestead if the probate judge declares the house homestead protected by creditors. Also, the house is protected if the Medicaid recipient is survived by a spouse, young child, or disabled child that resides in the house.

But what if the healthy spouse (also referred to as "community spouse") dies first? This is one of many reasons why engaging with an elder law attorney is highly recommended. An elder law attorney can walk you through the proper Medicaid-planning steps to protect the house and other assets, and otherwise minimize Medicaid's ability to engage in estate recovery.

Once useful tool to protect real estate from Medicaid Estate Recovery is known as a "Lady Bird Deed."

WHAT IS A LADY BIRD DEED?

A Lady Bird Deed is also known as an "Enhanced Life Estate Deed" (which is different than a Traditional Life Estate Deed).

This is an alternative way to transfer ownership of real estate outside of probate in Florida. Instead of transferring ownership/control of the real estate to the property owner's beneficiaries while the property owner is alive, a Lady Bird Deed allows the property owner to give themselves a life estate (also referred to as a life tenancy) and provides a remainder interest (usually to an heir, but it could be anyone the homeowner designates) after the homeowner dies.

Unlike a traditional life-estate deed or an outright transfer of property, the lady-bird deed provides that: (a) The life tenant has a right to sell or mortgage the entire property without joinder by the remainderman and retain all profits (can divest the remainderman of his/her interest); and (b) The life tenant can commit waste to the detriment to the remainderman.

Essentially, in an enhanced life estate deed, the life tenant does not owe the remainderman anything. The remainderman has absolutely no interest or rights to the real estate until the life tenant passes away.

Advantages of Using a Lady Bird Deed

The Lady Bird Deed / "enhanced life estate deed," is utilized to maintain control of the property, retaining the benefits of homestead (if applicable), and is used to avoid probate. It also has the advantage of allowing a homestead to retain its protected status from creditors.

If the deeded property is a homestead, there will be no loss of homestead tax exemption and the county will not reassess the property to raise taxes.

There are other tax advantages in utilizing a Lady Bird Deed, such as no additional documentary stamp taxes, which are beyond the scope of this article.

Advantages of Lady Bird Deed in a Medicaid Planning Context

Lady Bird Deeds do not assist in qualifying an applicant for Medicaid. But they do assist with minimizing Medicaid's right to estate recovery after the Medicaid recipient passes away. In a

Medicaid planning context, the Lady Bird Deed is a useful tool because it allows the real estate to avoid probate.

Lady Bird Deeds are not a gift or transfer, subject to a Medicaid disqualification penalty assessment; because the remainderman's right to the property can be taken away at any time (similar to how the owner of a life insurance contract can add, change or remove beneficiaries to life insurance proceeds at any time).

In fact, the Florida Medicaid manual specifically addresses Lady Bird Deeds as enhanced life estate deeds and tells the caseworker that they are legitimate and not to be considered a transfer of assets.

Let us look at how real estate, subject to a lady-bird deed, is handled in two contexts:

(1) Lady Bird Deed for Homestead

A home that is also deemed a Florida homestead property is (with few limitations related to specific debts that encumber the home) protected from creditors while the owner is alive and is similarly protected from attachment by creditors after they die.

Medicaid is treated as a general creditor. So, for a home that qualifies as an exempt homestead asset for Medicaid eligibility purposes, the primary benefit of using an enhanced life estate deed is primarily estate planning - i.e. get the home into the hands of your chosen beneficiary without them having to go through probate (which involves additional costs and time).

(2) Lady Bird Deed for Non-Homestead Properties

Second homes or income-producing properties are not protected by homestead in Florida. They may or may not be protected for Medicaid purposes (talk to your elder care lawyer to discuss strategies to ensure that they are). We know that rental properties are protected from being included as a Medicaid countable asset, but regardless, non-homestead properties are not granted the same protection from Medicaid Estate Recovery as homestead properties. Meaning, after the Medicaid recipient passes away, second homes or rental properties are likely at risk of being subject to Medicaid estate recovery.

However, a Lady Bird Deed can also protect against this threat.

Lady Bird Deeds let the non-homestead properties pass outside of probate. Since Medicaid Estate Recovery only applies to assets in the probatable estate, a huge problem is therefore solved.

Lady Bird Deed Risks

Generally, the risk with Lady Bird Deeds is that if the remainderman dies before the life tenant, the home will need to be probated and could therefore be subject to Medicaid Estate Recovery.

In addition, there are some mortgage lenders who will refuse to lend money on property subject to a lady-bird deed.

Finally, after the original owner has passed way, I have heard that some title companies will require a probate before insuring title on property transferred to an heir through a lady-bird deed.

These issues seem to be rare - but be sure to discuss these risks with your elder law attorney.

Some of my clients choose to utilize a Revocable Living Trust to hold property (homestead or non-homestead) because of its ability to avoid probate under multiple circumstances in ways that are more comprehensive and advantageous (can protect the property under a larger variety of circumstances compared to lady bird deeds).

BIG TAKEAWAY

Medicaid estate recovery is an issue to discuss with an elder law attorney. Usually, with proper planning, estate recover can be drastically minimized or eliminated altogether.

CHAPTER 9.

SOME LESSER KNOWN MEDICAID PROGRAMS THAT BENEFIT THE ELDERLY AND DISABLED.

Most Medicaid planning lawyers spend the vast majority of their time representing clients interested in obtaining or preserving Institutional Care Program Medicaid (for those needing skilled nursing facility level of care) and Home and Community Based Service Medicaid (for those who need extra help at home or in an ALF).

However, some Medicaid planning clients are looking to obtain or preserve their benefits from some lesser-known Medicaid programs focused on supporting Florida's elderly community. Typically, these clients come to me after being notified that they are about to receive an inheritance or personal injury settlement, and do not want to lose their Medicaid health insurance benefits.

Recall that some Medicaid programs allow transfers of assets/gifting without penalty, while others do not.

All qualification asset and income test standards noted in this chapter (and in this book) are current as of July 2023. All these numbers will change periodically.

The first two Medicaid programs fall under the "Community Medicaid for people aged 65 and over or the disabled" heading and consist of: Medically Needy and MEDS-AD (Medicaid for Aged and Disabled).

MEDICALLY NEEDY MEDICAID

The Medically Needy Medicaid program, also referred to as "share of cost" Medicaid, is for people who are elderly (65+) or disabled. Eligibility for the Medically Needy program requires that applicants have $5,000 (or less) in countable assets for an individual (or $6,000 for a couple). There is no specific income threshold (take monthly income and subtract $180.00), but the idea is that one's income is too high to qualify for other Medicaid programs, but too low to afford "allowable expenses," which include Medicare and other health insurance premiums, co-insurance payments, medical goods and services prescribed by a doctor, hospitalizations, prescription medicines, and medical transportation providers to obtain medical care - as long as all services are provided by enrolled Medicaid providers. For questions on what expenses count call DCF at 1-866-762-2237.

Medically Needy recipients cannot use over the counter medicines or supplies (e.g. aspirin or ace bandages) or non-health insurance premiums toward their share of cost.

What is the Share of Cost part of the Medically Needy Program?

The Medically Needy program is referred to as a "share of cost" because the Medicaid beneficiary must pay a portion of their income each month before Medicaid is approved. You can think of the share of cost as a deductible based on your family's monthly income and how much it exceeds traditional Medicaid income limits. So, you start each month <u>without</u> Medicaid health insurance coverage. Only when your allowable expenses equal your share of cost in any calendar month, will you be eligible for Medicaid for the rest of that same calendar month.

For example, if your share of cost is calculated at $675.00 and you go to the ER and receive a bill for $1,150, you would fax, mail, or walk that (and any other) bill into an ACCESS Florida office to prove that you have met your share of cost. Then Medicaid will pay the bill and any other allowable expenses for the rest of that month.

If your share of costs is $675.00 and you go to the doctor and only receive a bill for $150.00, you have not met your "share of cost" and you will have to pay that bill in full. However, if later in the same month you go to the hospital and receive a bill for $550.00, you would submit both bills to Medicaid (through ACCESS Florida) and the bill for $550.00 (and any allowable expenses incurred afterwards) would be covered by Medicaid.

On the first of the next calendar month, you start the Medically Needy share of cost calculation all over again.

MEDS-AD - MEDICAID FOR THE AGED AND DISABLED

For those who qualify (applicants must not have Medicare A or B), MEDS-AD will pay bills from doctors, hospitals, drug/prescription costs, PT, OT and short-term rehab stays.

If you are interested in these benefits, but have Medicare, see the QMB program described in the following pages.

MEDS-AD Medicaid Income and Asset Thresholds

Individuals can earn no more than $1,069.00 in monthly income (couples together can earn no more than $1,446.00/mo). Individuals must have no more than $5,000.00 in combined countable assets (couples = $6,000.00 in countable assets).

PACE - PROGRAM OF ALL-INCLUSIVE CARE FOR THE ELDERLY

PACE is a Medicare and Medicaid partnership. PACE eligibility requirements include being 55 or above and disabled, or 65 years or older. PACE must be the Medicare and Medicaid provider. PACE programs are organized around the local PACE Center and are designed to keep participants in the home or community as opposed to an institution. Financial Eligibility is similar to ICP/Long Term Care Medicaid Eligibility Requirements in Florida with no income restrictions for the well spouse only (asset test, income test, CSRA otherwise identical).

PACE centers provide: adult day care, doctor's offices, nursing services, social services, rehabilitation services, meals, recreational therapy, nutritional counseling, PT, OT, and more.

PACE is not currently available throughout Florida. Currently, PACE is available in Miami-Dade, only certain sections of Broward, Palm Beach, Pinellas, Lee, Collier, Clay, Duval and Charlotte counties.

PACE also pays for hospitalizations, regular doctors' visits, prescriptions, elder supplies such as diapers and wheelchairs, caregiver support, a portion of ALF, skilled rehab, and nursing home care.

PACE provides transportation to and from PACE facilities where they have activities for PACE members.

FLORIDA MEDICARE SAVINGS PROGRAMS

In Florida, there are several Medicaid benefits that fall under the category of "Medicare Savings Programs" - designed to pay for Medicare premiums, deductibles, coinsurance, and copayments for those who qualify. The Medicare Savings Programs addressed in this article include: Qualified Medicare Beneficiary (QMB); Special Low-Income Medicare Beneficiary (SLMB) and Qualifying Individuals (QI-1).

The QMB, SLMB and QI-1 Asset Limits are as follows:

Individual: $9,090.00

Couple: $13,630.00

QMB - Qualified Medicare Beneficiary

QMB Medicaid helps the elderly (or disabled) pay Medicare Part A premiums, Medicare Part B premiums, and accompanying deductibles, copays and most prescriptions (essentially all health-insurance related needs). To qualify, one must already be enrolled in Medicare Part A.

QMB asset limits are discussed above.

QMB Income Limits

Individual: $1,215.00/month

Couple: $1,643.00/month

SLMB - Special Low-Income Medicare Beneficiary

SLMB Medicaid helps those who qualify pay for Medicare Part B premiums only (i.e. the beneficiary must still pay Medicare Part A deductibles and coinsurance. SLMB asset limits are discussed above.

SLMB Income Limits

Individual: $1,458.00 | Couple: $1,972.00

QI-1 (Qualifying Individuals 1)

This Medicare Savings Plan may involve a waiting list and must be reapplied for every year (although those who were qualified in a prior year get preference). QI1 Asset Test limits are discussed above.

QI-1 Income Limits

Individual: $1,640.00 | Couple: $2,219.00

There are other Medicaid programs beyond the scope of this book.

PARTICIPANT DIRECTED OPTION (PDO)

PDO is related to the Medicaid Waiver / Home and Community Based Services Medicaid program (i.e. for those who want help paying for ALF or home-health care).

Generally, when my client has been approved for the Medicaid Waiver program, they will enroll in a Medicaid managed care organization (e.g. Humana, Sunshine Health, AETNA, Florida Community Care, etc...).

If my client desires care at home, the managed care plan will provide a list of home health agencies that are contracted with the organization. The assigned case manager will then approve a certain number of hours per day or per week.

IMPORTANT NOTE REGARDING

MEDICAID HOME-HEALTH CARE BENEFITS:

If Medicaid Waiver does not approve enough hours for the Medicaid recipient to safely remain at home (whether that home care is provided by a Medicaid-approved agency or a designated family member) that decision can be challenged.

An experienced Medicaid lawyer can assist with the appeal for additional home-care hours if needed.

However, for those who would prefer to receive their care from a friend, neighbor, family member, or other trusted caregiver (in lieu of going through a home-care agency), Florida Medicaid also offers the Participant Directed Option (PDO).

The only restriction is that your chosen paid care provider must be 18 years old or older, legally authorized to work in the United States, and able to pass a level 2 criminal background check.

They do not need any specific licensing or training to provide paid unskilled home care services.

However, once the care provider has passed the requirements, he/she can be paid (direct deposit) by the Medicaid managed care organization for the number of weekly hours approved.

The participant directed option (PDO), as of January 2024, pays a minimum wage of $15.00 per hour.

CHAPTER 10.

BENEFITS TO HAVING BOTH MEDICARE AND MEDICAID

When President Lyndon B. Johnson signed the legislation that established Medicare and Medicaid as two distinct programs, he likely did not consider the challenges that would arise among those eligible for both – a group that happens to have a significant need for consistent and comprehensive medical, behavioral and community social services.

Congress's attempt to bridge the gap in coordination of benefits (i.e. which program is supposed to provide which benefits and when) came in 2003 with the creation of the Dual-Eligible Special Needs Plan (D-SNP)[5].

DUAL-ENROLLED SPECIAL NEEDS PLAN (D-SNP)

---

[5] See Medicare Prescription Drug, Improvement and Modernization Act of 2003

Essentially, D-SNPs contract with Florida's Medicaid program to coordinate both Medicare and Medicaid benefits via a Medicare Advantage Plan. Every D-SNP must cover the same Medicare services that all Medicare Advantage plans are already required to provide - but will usually include bonus supplemental services on top.[6]

D-SNPs require the member to receive their prescription Part D benefits through their plan (they may not get a standalone Medicare prescription drug plan).

Becoming (or losing) dual eligibility will trigger a special enrollment period to choose a plan. Once enrolled, the D-SNP plan has 90 days to conduct a "Health Risk Assessment." It identifies the member's most urgent needs and creates an individualized care plan based on medical, functional, cognitive, psychosocial and mental health. All D-SNP members will have a PCP and care manager. But the care plan will incorporate an interdisciplinary team of specialists as needed.

After hospitalizations, members must receive a call within three days so the care manager can further explain and clarify the member's diagnosis and care instructions. In addition, the care manager will help coordinate follow-up appointments (including scheduling transportation), needed in-home care, and durable medical equipment.

What Additional Benefits Come with D-SNP Medicare/Medicaid Plans?

Some examples of additional assistance that may be included with D-SNPs, which we do not always see with traditional Medicare Advantage plans, include: a monetary allowance for over-the-counter supplies and utility bills (a cash benefit); allowance for the purchase of healthy foods (with more

---

[6]   https://www.medicare.gov/sign-upchange-plans/types-of-medicare-health-plans/how-medicare-special-needs-plans-snps-work

comprehensive diet and nutrition advice); allowance for fall prevention devices; additional social worker and behavioral services support; no referrals for providers/specialists in-network; expanded dental benefits; expanded hearing-aid and vision benefits (e.g. allowance for brand-name hearing aids and glasses); expanded non-emergency transportation; and $0.00 copay on prescriptions.

Essentially, D-SNP benefits can provide hundreds of dollars per month, or more, of potential additional benefits (in allowances and savings) compared to stand alone Medicare or Medicaid plans.

These expanded benefits can make a meaningful difference in the health and wellbeing of my client's lives, not to mention that it can help Floridians to remain at home longer (which is a goal of many people I speak to).

How to Qualify for a D-SNP Plan?

Essentially, to qualify for a Dual-Enrolled Special Needs Medicare Advantage Plan (D-SNP) one must qualify for both Medicare and Full-Medicaid, SLMB, QI, QMB (see Chapter 9) or Medicaid Waiver. There are other types of special needs Medicare advantage plans for those who are in a skilled nursing facility or with certain chronic conditions (which are beyond the scope of this book).

In addition, the type of Medicaid program you qualify for will determine whether there is any kind of limited cost sharing or no cost sharing at all.

For those who do not currently qualify for QMB or Medicaid Waiver but are seeing their healthcare bills or long-term care costs eating away at their life savings; an elder care lawyer / Medicaid-planning law firm can help you or your loved one qualify for these programs.

Once your elder law attorney protects your income and assets to get you qualified, this will then trigger the special Medicare enrollment period so you can take advantage of these expanded benefits.

CONCLUSION

As stated in the introduction, this book is not a comprehensive guide. It's essentially a Medicaid 101 long term care benefits primer.

It's just a starting point, not a "do it yourself" manual.

It is still necessary to meet with an experienced Elder Law attorney or Medicaid Lawyer to discuss your (or your loved one's) situation.

Some issues that are important but not covered in this book include, but are not limited to:

1. Additional and potentially valuable long-term care benefits available to Veterans through VA Improved Pension including Aid and Attendance.
2. Those who are, or became, disabled before turning 26 years old can take advantage of ABLE accounts to shelter a significant amount of additional money in a tax-advantaged manner.
3. Buying and selling real estate, in a Medicaid planning context, has all sorts of income tax, capital gains tax, and homestead implications.
4. There are Medicaid compliant annuities that are available – and may be useful with married couples.
5. There are differences between Medicaid Managed Care Organizations.
6. The long-term-care insurance partnership program allows a dollar-for-dollar Medicaid asset disregard for qualifying long-term-care insurance plans.

Medicaid planning requires a reassessment of current incapacity planning (durable power of attorney, health care surrogate designation) and estate planning needs (wills and trusts). As a result,

7. most of the frequently downloaded free durable power of attorney forms I see presented to me are <u>no good</u> for Medicaid planning purposes.

These, and other concepts, are not addressed in this book. The concepts that are addressed in this book are certainly not covered comprehensively. To do so would have made for a much longer volume.

Recall that from the beginning, I explained that this book's primary goal is to help you become a better advocate for yourself or the person you are trying to help.

If you have taken the time to read this book, you are ahead of the Medicaid game. You'll impress your elder law attorney with your level of knowledge that most potential clients just don't have. This book will equip you to ask better questions, better evaluate Medicaid planning strategies presented to you and, hopefully, make better decisions.

The most difficult aspect of my job is that very few people know that Medicaid planning even exists, so they don't always think to ask about it. I try to lecture, put on webinars, and broadcast information in the form of articles, blogs, and videos - anything to try to get the word out that you don't have to spend all your hard-earned money before asking the government for assistance.

If you are anywhere in Florida and are interested in an Elder Law, Medicaid Planning, Estate Planning or Probate consultation, my team can be reached by filling out a form at ElderNeedsLaw.com or you can call our Central Scheduling line: (786) 756-8169.

I encourage you to check out and subscribe to our YouTube Channel, where we regularly post practical and informative videos answering people's questions and interviewing other senior-oriented resources:

www.youtube.com/@elderneedslaw

If you are not in Florida, you may also reach out to me, and I would be happy to refer you to a colleague in another state.

Alternatively, you can reach out to the National Academy of Elder Law Attorneys (www.naela.org/) to find someone in your area.

What I love about Elder Law is that it allows me to empower my older or disabled clients to gain access to resources that allow them to experience a higher quality of life up until the very end.

Thank you for your interest and for reading this book.

I wish you and your family the very best.

ABOUT THE AUTHOR: JASON NEUFELD

Jason Neufeld, Esq. is the founding partner of Elder Needs Law, PLLC, with physical offices in Aventura, Plantation, and Boca Raton (with additional satellite offices available and serving clients remotely statewide).

Elder Needs Law, PLLC focuses on Medicaid Asset Protection Planning, Estate Planning, Probate, and other elder-related issues such as special needs planning and guardianship.

Jason is a "AV" preeminent rated attorney by Martindale-Hubbell as a "Platinum Client Champion" and is consistently recognized as a top lawyer among his peers between Super Lawyers and Legal Trends Legal Elite Magazines (2012-2024).

Jason is proud to serve on the Board of Directors, and Executive Committee for the Academy of Florida Elder Law Attorneys, is the Co-Chair of the Broward County Bar Association Elder Law Section and serves on several committees with the Florida Bar Elder Law Section as well as the Miami-Dade Mayor's Initiative on Aging.

Jason regularly guest lectures/presents at a variety of educational events throughout Florida, including caregiver support groups and elder law conferences where he teaches and learns from other elder law attorneys.

Jason also authors articles in elder law trade publications to educate other elder law attorneys. He is especially proud to publish articles and videos to provide free and practical educational content for the benefit of all elderly and disabled Floridians on his popular blog and YouTube channel.

Jason lives in South Florida with his wife, Marla, and their twin boys, Ethan and Asher.

Connect with Jason / Elder Needs Law on Social!

Youtube.com/@elderneedslaw

Facebook.com/elderneedslaw

Linkedin.com/in/elder-law-attorney

Tiktok.com/@elderneedslaw

Made in the USA
Monee, IL
13 July 2024

61762724R00056